50 Cozy Days Meals

By: Kelly Johnson

Table of Contents

- Chicken Pot Pie
- Beef Stew
- Creamy Tomato Soup with Grilled Cheese
- Macaroni and Cheese
- Slow Cooker Chili
- Baked Ziti
- Shepherd's Pie
- Chicken and Rice Casserole
- Meatloaf with Mashed Potatoes
- Lasagna
- Beef and Vegetable Soup
- Roasted Chicken with Root Vegetables
- Butternut Squash Soup
- Chicken Alfredo
- Biscuits and Gravy
- Stuffed Bell Peppers
- Mushroom Risotto
- Sloppy Joes
- Potato Leek Soup
- Chicken Noodle Soup
- Beef Stroganoff
- Pulled Pork Sandwiches
- Baked Mac and Cheese with Bacon
- Broccoli and Cheddar Stuffed Chicken
- Creamy Spinach and Artichoke Dip
- Homemade Meatballs in Marinara Sauce
- Creamy Potato Soup
- Sausage and Sauerkraut
- Roasted Butternut Squash and Sage Pasta
- Fish Tacos with Cabbage Slaw
- Chicken Enchiladas
- Sweet Potato and Black Bean Chili
- Eggplant Parmesan
- French Onion Soup
- Sausage and Pepper Skillet

- Chicken Parmesan
- Creamy Polenta with Mushrooms
- Spaghetti and Meatballs
- Risotto with Shrimp and Peas
- Roasted Chicken Thighs with Brussels Sprouts
- Vegetable Frittata
- Roast Beef with Yorkshire Pudding
- Bacon-Wrapped Pork Tenderloin
- Beef and Barley Soup
- Pork and Apple Stew
- Braised Short Ribs
- Chicken and Dumplings
- Sautéed Brussels Sprouts with Bacon
- Pumpkin Risotto
- Tofu Stir-Fry with Rice

Chicken Pot Pie

Ingredients:

- 2 cups cooked chicken (diced)
- 1 cup frozen mixed vegetables (carrots, peas, corn, etc.)
- 1/2 cup onion (chopped)
- 1/2 cup butter
- 1/4 cup flour
- 2 cups chicken broth
- 1 cup milk
- 1 teaspoon thyme
- Salt and pepper to taste
- 1 package pie crusts (or homemade)

Instructions:

1. **Prepare Filling:** In a large skillet, melt butter and sauté onions until soft. Add flour and cook for 1 minute. Slowly whisk in the chicken broth and milk, cooking until the mixture thickens. Add chicken, mixed vegetables, thyme, salt, and pepper. Remove from heat.
2. **Assemble Pie:** Preheat oven to 375°F (190°C). Roll out one pie crust and line a pie dish. Pour the filling into the crust. Top with the second crust, sealing edges and cutting slits in the top.
3. **Bake:** Bake for 30-35 minutes until golden brown. Let cool slightly before serving.

Beef Stew

Ingredients:

- 1 lb beef stew meat (cubed)
- 1 onion (chopped)
- 2 carrots (sliced)
- 2 potatoes (diced)
- 2 cups beef broth
- 2 cups water
- 1/2 cup red wine (optional)
- 2 cloves garlic (minced)
- 2 tablespoons tomato paste
- 1 teaspoon dried thyme
- Salt and pepper to taste

Instructions:

1. **Brown Beef:** In a large pot, brown beef cubes in a little oil. Remove and set aside.
2. **Cook Veggies:** In the same pot, sauté onion, garlic, carrots, and potatoes until soft. Add tomato paste and cook for 2 minutes.
3. **Simmer Stew:** Return beef to the pot and add broth, water, wine, thyme, salt, and pepper. Bring to a boil, then simmer for 1-2 hours until beef is tender.
4. **Serve:** Adjust seasoning and serve hot.

Creamy Tomato Soup with Grilled Cheese

Ingredients:

- 1 can (28 oz) crushed tomatoes
- 1 cup heavy cream
- 1 onion (chopped)
- 2 cloves garlic (minced)
- 2 tablespoons olive oil
- Salt and pepper to taste
- 4 slices of bread
- 2 tablespoons butter
- 4 slices of cheddar cheese

Instructions:

1. **Make Soup:** Heat olive oil in a pot and sauté onions and garlic until soft. Add tomatoes and simmer for 15-20 minutes. Use an immersion blender to puree the soup until smooth. Stir in heavy cream, salt, and pepper.
2. **Make Grilled Cheese:** Butter bread slices and place cheese between two slices. Grill in a pan over medium heat until golden and the cheese is melted.
3. **Serve:** Serve the tomato soup with the grilled cheese sandwich on the side.

Macaroni and Cheese

Ingredients:

- 8 oz elbow macaroni
- 2 cups shredded cheddar cheese
- 1 cup milk
- 1/4 cup butter
- 2 tablespoons flour
- 1/2 teaspoon garlic powder
- Salt and pepper to taste

Instructions:

1. **Cook Pasta:** Boil macaroni according to package instructions. Drain and set aside.
2. **Make Cheese Sauce:** In a saucepan, melt butter over medium heat. Stir in flour and cook for 1-2 minutes. Slowly whisk in milk and cook until the sauce thickens. Add cheese, garlic powder, salt, and pepper, stirring until melted.
3. **Combine:** Mix the cooked macaroni with the cheese sauce. Serve warm.

Slow Cooker Chili

Ingredients:

- 1 lb ground beef or turkey
- 1 onion (chopped)
- 1 bell pepper (chopped)
- 2 cloves garlic (minced)
- 1 can (15 oz) kidney beans (drained and rinsed)
- 1 can (15 oz) diced tomatoes
- 1 can (6 oz) tomato paste
- 2 tablespoons chili powder
- 1 teaspoon cumin
- Salt and pepper to taste

Instructions:

1. **Brown Meat:** In a skillet, brown the meat with onion, bell pepper, and garlic. Drain excess fat.
2. **Slow Cook:** Transfer the meat mixture to a slow cooker. Add beans, tomatoes, tomato paste, chili powder, cumin, salt, and pepper. Stir well.
3. **Cook:** Cover and cook on low for 6-8 hours or high for 3-4 hours. Serve with toppings like cheese or sour cream if desired.

Baked Ziti

Ingredients:

- 1 lb ziti pasta
- 3 cups marinara sauce
- 2 cups ricotta cheese
- 2 cups shredded mozzarella cheese
- 1/4 cup grated Parmesan cheese
- 1 teaspoon dried basil
- Salt and pepper to taste

Instructions:

1. **Cook Pasta:** Cook ziti according to package instructions, then drain.
2. **Assemble Dish:** Preheat oven to 375°F (190°C). In a large bowl, mix pasta, marinara sauce, ricotta, mozzarella, Parmesan, basil, salt, and pepper.
3. **Bake:** Pour the mixture into a baking dish and top with additional mozzarella cheese. Bake for 20-25 minutes, until bubbly and golden.

Shepherd's Pie

Ingredients:

- 1 lb ground lamb or beef
- 1 onion (chopped)
- 2 carrots (diced)
- 1 cup peas
- 1 cup beef broth
- 2 tablespoons tomato paste
- 4 cups mashed potatoes (prepared)
- 2 tablespoons butter
- Salt and pepper to taste

Instructions:

1. **Cook Filling:** Brown meat in a pan with onions, carrots, and peas. Stir in tomato paste and broth, and simmer for 10 minutes.
2. **Assemble:** Preheat oven to 400°F (200°C). Transfer the meat mixture to a baking dish and top with mashed potatoes.
3. **Bake:** Dot with butter and bake for 20 minutes, until the top is golden.

Chicken and Rice Casserole

Ingredients:

- 2 cups cooked chicken (shredded)
- 1 cup cooked rice
- 1 can (10 oz) cream of chicken soup
- 1/2 cup milk
- 1 cup shredded cheddar cheese
- Salt and pepper to taste

Instructions:

1. **Mix Ingredients:** Preheat oven to 350°F (175°C). In a large bowl, mix chicken, rice, soup, milk, and cheese.
2. **Bake:** Pour mixture into a greased baking dish and bake for 25-30 minutes, until bubbly.

Meatloaf with Mashed Potatoes

Ingredients:

- 1 lb ground beef
- 1 egg
- 1 cup breadcrumbs
- 1/2 cup milk
- 1 onion (chopped)
- 1 tablespoon Worcestershire sauce
- 1/4 cup ketchup
- Salt and pepper to taste
- 4 cups mashed potatoes

Instructions:

1. **Make Meatloaf:** Preheat oven to 350°F (175°C). In a bowl, mix beef, egg, breadcrumbs, milk, onion, Worcestershire sauce, salt, and pepper. Form into a loaf and place in a baking dish.
2. **Bake:** Top with ketchup and bake for 50-60 minutes.
3. **Serve:** Serve with mashed potatoes on the side.

Lasagna

Ingredients:

- 1 lb ground beef
- 1 onion (chopped)
- 2 cloves garlic (minced)
- 1 jar marinara sauce
- 12 lasagna noodles (cooked)
- 1 cup ricotta cheese
- 2 cups shredded mozzarella cheese
- 1/4 cup grated Parmesan cheese
- 2 teaspoons dried basil
- 1 teaspoon dried oregano
- Salt and pepper to taste

Instructions:

1. **Cook Meat:** Brown the ground beef with onion and garlic in a large skillet. Drain excess fat. Add marinara sauce, basil, oregano, salt, and pepper. Simmer for 10 minutes.
2. **Assemble Lasagna:** Preheat oven to 375°F (190°C). In a baking dish, spread a thin layer of sauce. Layer cooked lasagna noodles, ricotta cheese, sauce, mozzarella, and Parmesan. Repeat layers until ingredients are used up, finishing with sauce and cheese on top.
3. **Bake:** Cover with foil and bake for 25 minutes. Remove foil and bake for an additional 15-20 minutes until bubbly. Let rest before serving.

Beef and Vegetable Soup

Ingredients:

- 1 lb beef stew meat (cubed)
- 1 onion (chopped)
- 2 carrots (diced)
- 2 potatoes (diced)
- 1 celery stalk (chopped)
- 1 can (14 oz) diced tomatoes
- 4 cups beef broth
- 2 cloves garlic (minced)
- 1 teaspoon dried thyme
- Salt and pepper to taste

Instructions:

1. **Brown Beef:** In a large pot, brown the beef stew meat. Remove and set aside.
2. **Cook Veggies:** In the same pot, sauté onions, carrots, celery, and garlic until softened. Add potatoes and beef broth, then return the beef to the pot.
3. **Simmer Soup:** Add thyme, salt, and pepper, and bring to a boil. Reduce heat and simmer for 1-1.5 hours until beef and vegetables are tender. Adjust seasoning and serve warm.

Roasted Chicken with Root Vegetables

Ingredients:

- 1 whole chicken (3-4 lbs)
- 2 tablespoons olive oil
- 1 tablespoon lemon juice
- 2 teaspoons dried rosemary
- 1 teaspoon garlic powder
- Salt and pepper to taste
- 4 carrots (peeled and cut into chunks)
- 4 potatoes (cut into chunks)
- 2 parsnips (peeled and cut into chunks)
- 1 onion (quartered)

Instructions:

1. **Prepare Chicken:** Preheat oven to 400°F (200°C). Rub the chicken with olive oil, lemon juice, rosemary, garlic powder, salt, and pepper.
2. **Roast Chicken:** Place the chicken in the center of a roasting pan and arrange the root vegetables around it.
3. **Cook:** Roast for 1-1.5 hours, or until the chicken reaches 165°F (75°C) and vegetables are tender. Let rest for 10 minutes before carving.

Butternut Squash Soup

Ingredients:

- 1 medium butternut squash (peeled, seeded, and cubed)
- 1 onion (chopped)
- 2 cloves garlic (minced)
- 4 cups vegetable broth
- 1/2 teaspoon ground cinnamon
- 1/4 teaspoon nutmeg
- 1/2 cup heavy cream
- Salt and pepper to taste

Instructions:

1. **Cook Veggies:** In a large pot, sauté onion and garlic in olive oil until softened. Add cubed squash and cook for 5 minutes.
2. **Simmer Soup:** Add vegetable broth, cinnamon, nutmeg, salt, and pepper. Bring to a boil, then reduce heat and simmer for 20-25 minutes, until squash is tender.
3. **Blend:** Use an immersion blender to puree the soup until smooth. Stir in heavy cream and adjust seasoning. Serve hot.

Chicken Alfredo

Ingredients:

- 2 chicken breasts (boneless, skinless)
- 1 tablespoon olive oil
- 2 cloves garlic (minced)
- 1 cup heavy cream
- 1 cup grated Parmesan cheese
- 8 oz fettuccine pasta
- 2 tablespoons butter
- Salt and pepper to taste

Instructions:

1. **Cook Chicken:** Season chicken breasts with salt and pepper. Cook in olive oil in a large skillet over medium heat for 6-7 minutes per side, until cooked through. Remove and slice thinly.
2. **Make Alfredo Sauce:** In the same skillet, melt butter and sauté garlic for 1 minute. Add heavy cream and bring to a simmer. Stir in Parmesan cheese and cook until the sauce thickens.
3. **Combine:** Cook fettuccine pasta according to package instructions. Drain and toss with Alfredo sauce and sliced chicken. Serve immediately.

Biscuits and Gravy

Ingredients:

- 1 can refrigerated biscuit dough (or homemade biscuits)
- 1 lb sausage (ground)
- 2 tablespoons flour
- 2 cups milk
- Salt and pepper to taste

Instructions:

1. **Bake Biscuits:** Preheat oven and bake biscuits according to package instructions.
2. **Cook Sausage:** In a skillet, cook the sausage over medium heat, breaking it up until browned. Sprinkle in flour and stir to combine.
3. **Make Gravy:** Slowly add milk, stirring constantly until the gravy thickens. Season with salt and pepper.
4. **Serve:** Serve sausage gravy over warm biscuits.

Stuffed Bell Peppers

Ingredients:

- 4 bell peppers (tops cut off, seeded)
- 1 lb ground beef
- 1 onion (chopped)
- 1 cup cooked rice
- 1 can (14.5 oz) diced tomatoes
- 1 teaspoon garlic powder
- 1 teaspoon Italian seasoning
- Salt and pepper to taste
- 1 cup shredded mozzarella cheese

Instructions:

1. **Prepare Peppers:** Preheat oven to 375°F (190°C). Place the peppers in a baking dish and set aside.
2. **Cook Filling:** In a skillet, brown ground beef with onion. Stir in rice, tomatoes, garlic powder, Italian seasoning, salt, and pepper.
3. **Stuff Peppers:** Stuff each pepper with the beef mixture. Top with mozzarella cheese.
4. **Bake:** Cover with foil and bake for 25-30 minutes. Remove foil and bake for an additional 10 minutes until the cheese is melted and bubbly.

Mushroom Risotto

Ingredients:

- 1 cup Arborio rice
- 2 cups chicken or vegetable broth
- 1 cup white wine
- 1/2 cup Parmesan cheese
- 2 cups mushrooms (sliced)
- 1 onion (chopped)
- 2 tablespoons butter
- Salt and pepper to taste

Instructions:

1. **Sauté Veggies:** In a large pan, melt butter and sauté onions until translucent. Add mushrooms and cook until soft.
2. **Cook Rice:** Add Arborio rice and cook for 1-2 minutes. Slowly add wine, stirring constantly. Gradually add broth, 1/2 cup at a time, stirring until absorbed before adding more. Continue until rice is tender and creamy (about 20 minutes).
3. **Finish:** Stir in Parmesan cheese, salt, and pepper. Serve immediately.

Sloppy Joes

Ingredients:

- 1 lb ground beef
- 1 onion (chopped)
- 1 bell pepper (chopped)
- 1 can (15 oz) tomato sauce
- 2 tablespoons ketchup
- 1 tablespoon Worcestershire sauce
- 1 teaspoon chili powder
- Salt and pepper to taste
- 4 hamburger buns

Instructions:

1. **Cook Meat:** In a large skillet, brown ground beef with onion and bell pepper. Drain excess fat.
2. **Make Sauce:** Stir in tomato sauce, ketchup, Worcestershire sauce, chili powder, salt, and pepper. Simmer for 10-15 minutes.
3. **Serve:** Spoon the mixture onto hamburger buns and serve.

Potato Leek Soup

Ingredients:

- 3 large potatoes (peeled and diced)
- 2 leeks (cleaned and chopped)
- 1 medium onion (chopped)
- 2 cloves garlic (minced)
- 4 cups vegetable broth
- 1 cup heavy cream
- 2 tablespoons butter
- Salt and pepper to taste

Instructions:

1. **Sauté Veggies:** In a large pot, melt butter and sauté onions, leeks, and garlic until softened (about 5-7 minutes).
2. **Cook Potatoes:** Add the diced potatoes and vegetable broth. Bring to a boil, then reduce to a simmer for 15-20 minutes, until potatoes are tender.
3. **Blend Soup:** Use an immersion blender to puree the soup until smooth, or leave it slightly chunky for texture. Stir in heavy cream and season with salt and pepper.
4. **Serve:** Serve hot with fresh bread.

Chicken Noodle Soup

Ingredients:

- 2 chicken breasts (boneless, skinless)
- 6 cups chicken broth
- 2 carrots (sliced)
- 2 celery stalks (sliced)
- 1 medium onion (chopped)
- 2 cloves garlic (minced)
- 1 teaspoon dried thyme
- 1 teaspoon dried parsley
- Salt and pepper to taste
- 1 1/2 cups egg noodles

Instructions:

1. **Cook Chicken:** In a large pot, cook chicken breasts in chicken broth until fully cooked. Remove and shred the chicken.
2. **Cook Veggies:** Add carrots, celery, onion, garlic, thyme, parsley, salt, and pepper to the pot. Simmer for 10-15 minutes.
3. **Add Noodles:** Add egg noodles to the pot and cook until tender, about 8-10 minutes.
4. **Finish Soup:** Return shredded chicken to the soup. Adjust seasoning and serve warm.

Beef Stroganoff

Ingredients:

- 1 lb beef (sirloin or tenderloin, sliced into strips)
- 1 onion (chopped)
- 2 cloves garlic (minced)
- 1 cup mushrooms (sliced)
- 1 cup beef broth
- 1/2 cup sour cream
- 1 tablespoon flour
- 2 tablespoons butter
- Salt and pepper to taste
- 1 teaspoon Worcestershire sauce
- 2 cups egg noodles (cooked)

Instructions:

1. **Sear Beef:** In a large skillet, melt butter and sear the beef strips until browned. Remove and set aside.
2. **Sauté Veggies:** In the same skillet, sauté onion, garlic, and mushrooms until softened.
3. **Make Sauce:** Sprinkle flour over the veggies and stir to combine. Gradually add beef broth, Worcestershire sauce, salt, and pepper. Bring to a simmer and cook until thickened (about 5 minutes).
4. **Finish:** Stir in sour cream and return beef to the skillet. Cook for 2-3 more minutes. Serve over egg noodles.

Pulled Pork Sandwiches

Ingredients:

- 3-4 lbs pork shoulder (boneless)
- 1 cup BBQ sauce
- 1/4 cup apple cider vinegar
- 1 tablespoon brown sugar
- 1 teaspoon paprika
- 1 teaspoon garlic powder
- Salt and pepper to taste
- 8 hamburger buns

Instructions:

1. **Prepare Pork:** Rub the pork shoulder with paprika, garlic powder, salt, and pepper.
2. **Slow Cook:** Place the pork in a slow cooker with BBQ sauce, apple cider vinegar, and brown sugar. Cook on low for 8-10 hours, or until the meat is tender and easily shreds.
3. **Shred Pork:** Remove pork from the slow cooker, shred with two forks, and return to the sauce.
4. **Serve:** Pile the pulled pork onto hamburger buns and serve with extra BBQ sauce if desired.

Baked Mac and Cheese with Bacon

Ingredients:

- 8 oz elbow macaroni (cooked)
- 2 cups shredded cheddar cheese
- 1 cup grated Parmesan cheese
- 2 cups milk
- 2 tablespoons butter
- 2 tablespoons flour
- 1/2 teaspoon garlic powder
- Salt and pepper to taste
- 1/2 cup cooked bacon (crumbled)
- 1/2 cup breadcrumbs (for topping)

Instructions:

1. **Make Cheese Sauce:** In a saucepan, melt butter and stir in flour to create a roux. Gradually add milk, whisking constantly until smooth. Stir in cheddar cheese, Parmesan, garlic powder, salt, and pepper.
2. **Combine Pasta:** In a large bowl, mix the cooked macaroni with the cheese sauce and crumbled bacon.
3. **Bake:** Transfer to a greased baking dish, top with breadcrumbs, and bake at 350°F (175°C) for 20-25 minutes, or until bubbly and golden.

Broccoli and Cheddar Stuffed Chicken

Ingredients:

- 4 boneless, skinless chicken breasts
- 1 cup broccoli (steamed and chopped)
- 1 cup shredded cheddar cheese
- 1/4 cup cream cheese
- 1 teaspoon garlic powder
- Salt and pepper to taste
- 1 tablespoon olive oil

Instructions:

1. **Prepare Filling:** In a bowl, mix the steamed broccoli, cheddar cheese, cream cheese, garlic powder, salt, and pepper.
2. **Stuff Chicken:** Cut a pocket into each chicken breast and stuff with the broccoli and cheese mixture.
3. **Cook Chicken:** Heat olive oil in a skillet and cook the chicken for 6-7 minutes per side, until golden and cooked through (165°F/75°C).
4. **Serve:** Serve hot with your choice of side dishes.

Creamy Spinach and Artichoke Dip

Ingredients:

- 1 can (14 oz) artichoke hearts (drained and chopped)
- 1 cup frozen spinach (thawed and drained)
- 1/2 cup cream cheese
- 1/2 cup sour cream
- 1/4 cup grated Parmesan cheese
- 1 cup shredded mozzarella cheese
- 1/2 teaspoon garlic powder
- Salt and pepper to taste

Instructions:

1. **Mix Ingredients:** In a bowl, combine artichokes, spinach, cream cheese, sour cream, Parmesan, mozzarella, garlic powder, salt, and pepper.
2. **Bake Dip:** Transfer to a baking dish and bake at 375°F (190°C) for 20-25 minutes until bubbly and golden on top.
3. **Serve:** Serve with tortilla chips or sliced baguette for dipping.

Homemade Meatballs in Marinara Sauce

Ingredients:

- 1 lb ground beef
- 1/4 cup breadcrumbs
- 1/4 cup grated Parmesan cheese
- 1 egg
- 2 cloves garlic (minced)
- 1 teaspoon dried basil
- 1 teaspoon dried oregano
- Salt and pepper to taste
- 2 cups marinara sauce

Instructions:

1. **Make Meatballs:** Preheat oven to 375°F (190°C). In a bowl, combine beef, breadcrumbs, Parmesan, egg, garlic, basil, oregano, salt, and pepper. Form into meatballs and place on a baking sheet.
2. **Cook Meatballs:** Bake meatballs for 15-20 minutes, or until cooked through.
3. **Simmer in Sauce:** Heat marinara sauce in a large pot. Add meatballs and simmer for 10-15 minutes.
4. **Serve:** Serve meatballs with pasta or on a sub roll.

Creamy Potato Soup

Ingredients:

- 4 large potatoes (peeled and diced)
- 1 onion (chopped)
- 2 cloves garlic (minced)
- 4 cups chicken broth
- 1 cup heavy cream
- 2 tablespoons butter
- 1 teaspoon dried thyme
- Salt and pepper to taste

Instructions:

1. **Cook Veggies:** In a large pot, sauté onions and garlic in butter until softened. Add diced potatoes and chicken broth. Bring to a boil, then reduce heat and simmer for 15-20 minutes, until potatoes are tender.
2. **Blend Soup:** Use an immersion blender to blend the soup until smooth (optional: leave some chunks for texture).
3. **Add Cream:** Stir in heavy cream, thyme, salt, and pepper. Simmer for 5 more minutes.
4. **Serve:** Serve with crumbled bacon, shredded cheese, or chives.

Sausage and Sauerkraut

Ingredients:

- 4 sausages (bratwurst or Italian, your choice)
- 1 medium onion (sliced)
- 2 cups sauerkraut (drained and rinsed)
- 1/2 cup beer (or water)
- 1 tablespoon mustard (optional)
- 1 tablespoon olive oil
- Salt and pepper to taste

Instructions:

1. **Cook Sausages:** In a large skillet, heat olive oil and cook sausages over medium heat until browned and cooked through (about 8-10 minutes). Remove and set aside.
2. **Sauté Onions:** In the same skillet, add onions and sauté until softened (about 5 minutes).
3. **Simmer Sauerkraut:** Add sauerkraut to the skillet with the onions, pour in the beer (or water), and simmer for 5 minutes.
4. **Combine:** Return sausages to the skillet and cook for an additional 5 minutes, allowing flavors to meld.
5. **Serve:** Serve the sausages with the sauerkraut and a dollop of mustard, if desired.

Roasted Butternut Squash and Sage Pasta

Ingredients:

- 1 medium butternut squash (peeled, seeded, and diced)
- 12 oz pasta (such as penne or fettuccine)
- 1 tablespoon olive oil
- 1 tablespoon butter
- 2 tablespoons fresh sage (chopped)
- 1/2 cup Parmesan cheese (grated)
- 1/2 cup heavy cream
- Salt and pepper to taste

Instructions:

1. **Roast Squash:** Preheat oven to 400°F (200°C). Toss diced butternut squash with olive oil, salt, and pepper. Spread on a baking sheet and roast for 20-25 minutes until tender.
2. **Cook Pasta:** Cook pasta according to package instructions. Drain and set aside, reserving 1/2 cup of pasta water.
3. **Make Sauce:** In a skillet, melt butter over medium heat. Add fresh sage and sauté for 1 minute. Stir in heavy cream and Parmesan, and simmer for 2-3 minutes.
4. **Combine:** Add the roasted squash and pasta to the skillet, tossing to coat. Add reserved pasta water to loosen the sauce if needed.
5. **Serve:** Serve hot, garnished with extra Parmesan and fresh sage.

Fish Tacos with Cabbage Slaw

Ingredients:

- 1 lb white fish fillets (such as tilapia or cod)
- 1 tablespoon olive oil
- 1 teaspoon chili powder
- 1 teaspoon cumin
- 1/2 teaspoon garlic powder
- 8 small corn tortillas
- 1 cup shredded cabbage
- 1/4 cup sour cream
- 2 tablespoons lime juice
- Salt and pepper to taste

Instructions:

1. **Season Fish:** Rub the fish fillets with olive oil, chili powder, cumin, garlic powder, salt, and pepper.
2. **Cook Fish:** Heat a skillet over medium heat and cook the fish for 3-4 minutes per side, until cooked through and flaky.
3. **Make Slaw:** In a bowl, mix the shredded cabbage with sour cream, lime juice, salt, and pepper.
4. **Assemble Tacos:** Warm the tortillas in a dry skillet. Flake the fish into pieces and place on the tortillas. Top with cabbage slaw.
5. **Serve:** Serve with lime wedges and optional toppings like avocado or salsa.

Chicken Enchiladas

Ingredients:

- 2 chicken breasts (cooked and shredded)
- 1 cup enchilada sauce (red or green)
- 10 corn tortillas
- 1 cup shredded cheese (cheddar or Mexican blend)
- 1/2 onion (chopped)
- 1/4 cup cilantro (chopped)
- 1 teaspoon cumin
- Salt and pepper to taste

Instructions:

1. **Prepare Filling:** Preheat oven to 375°F (190°C). In a bowl, combine shredded chicken, 1/2 cup enchilada sauce, cumin, salt, and pepper.
2. **Assemble Enchiladas:** Heat tortillas slightly to soften. Spread a spoonful of the chicken mixture down the center of each tortilla, top with cheese, and roll up.
3. **Bake:** Place the rolled enchiladas in a baking dish. Pour the remaining enchilada sauce over the top and sprinkle with extra cheese.
4. **Bake:** Bake for 20-25 minutes, until cheese is melted and bubbly.
5. **Serve:** Garnish with chopped onions and cilantro.

Sweet Potato and Black Bean Chili

Ingredients:

- 2 medium sweet potatoes (peeled and diced)
- 1 can (15 oz) black beans (rinsed and drained)
- 1 onion (chopped)
- 2 cloves garlic (minced)
- 1 can (14 oz) diced tomatoes
- 1 tablespoon chili powder
- 1 teaspoon cumin
- 1 teaspoon smoked paprika
- 1/2 teaspoon cinnamon (optional)
- 3 cups vegetable broth
- Salt and pepper to taste

Instructions:

1. **Sauté Vegetables:** In a large pot, heat oil over medium heat and sauté onion and garlic until softened.
2. **Cook Sweet Potatoes:** Add sweet potatoes, black beans, diced tomatoes, chili powder, cumin, smoked paprika, and cinnamon (if using).
3. **Simmer:** Add vegetable broth and bring to a boil. Reduce heat and simmer for 30 minutes, or until sweet potatoes are tender.
4. **Serve:** Season with salt and pepper. Serve hot, topped with optional toppings like sour cream or cilantro.

Eggplant Parmesan

Ingredients:

- 2 medium eggplants (sliced into rounds)
- 2 cups marinara sauce
- 1 cup breadcrumbs
- 1 cup shredded mozzarella cheese
- 1/2 cup grated Parmesan cheese
- 1 egg (beaten)
- 1/4 cup fresh basil (chopped)
- Olive oil for frying
- Salt and pepper to taste

Instructions:

1. **Bread Eggplant:** Dip eggplant slices into beaten egg, then coat with breadcrumbs.
2. **Fry Eggplant:** Heat olive oil in a skillet over medium heat and fry eggplant slices until golden and crispy, about 2-3 minutes per side.
3. **Assemble Dish:** Preheat oven to 375°F (190°C). Spread marinara sauce in the bottom of a baking dish. Layer fried eggplant, mozzarella, and Parmesan, and repeat layers.
4. **Bake:** Bake for 20 minutes, until cheese is bubbly and golden.
5. **Serve:** Garnish with fresh basil and serve hot.

French Onion Soup

Ingredients:

- 4 large onions (thinly sliced)
- 2 tablespoons butter
- 1 teaspoon sugar
- 4 cups beef broth
- 1 cup white wine
- 2 cloves garlic (minced)
- 2 sprigs thyme
- 1 baguette (sliced)
- 1 1/2 cups Gruyère cheese (grated)
- Salt and pepper to taste

Instructions:

1. **Caramelize Onions:** In a large pot, melt butter over medium heat. Add onions, sugar, salt, and pepper, and cook until caramelized, about 30 minutes.
2. **Add Liquids:** Stir in garlic, wine, and thyme, and cook for 5 minutes. Add beef broth and simmer for 20 minutes.
3. **Prepare Bread:** Toast baguette slices and top with Gruyère cheese.
4. **Finish Soup:** Ladle soup into oven-safe bowls, place a slice of bread on top, and sprinkle with cheese.
5. **Broil:** Broil for 2-3 minutes until cheese is melted and golden.
6. **Serve:** Serve hot with a sprinkle of thyme.

Sausage and Pepper Skillet

Ingredients:

- 4 sausages (Italian or your choice)
- 2 bell peppers (sliced)
- 1 onion (sliced)
- 2 cloves garlic (minced)
- 1 tablespoon olive oil
- Salt and pepper to taste

Instructions:

1. **Cook Sausages:** Heat olive oil in a skillet over medium heat and cook sausages until browned and cooked through, about 8-10 minutes.
2. **Sauté Veggies:** Remove sausages and add bell peppers, onion, and garlic to the skillet. Cook until softened, about 5-7 minutes.
3. **Combine:** Slice sausages and return to the skillet.
4. **Serve:** Toss everything together and serve hot.

Chicken Parmesan

Ingredients:

- 4 chicken breasts (boneless, skinless)
- 1 cup breadcrumbs
- 1 cup marinara sauce
- 1 cup shredded mozzarella cheese
- 1/4 cup grated Parmesan cheese
- 1 egg (beaten)
- Salt and pepper to taste

Instructions:

1. **Bread Chicken:** Preheat oven to 375°F (190°C). Dip chicken breasts in beaten egg, then coat in breadcrumbs.
2. **Cook Chicken:** Heat oil in a skillet and cook chicken for 4-5 minutes per side, until golden.
3. **Assemble:** Place chicken in a baking dish, top with marinara sauce, mozzarella, and Parmesan.
4. **Bake:** Bake for 20 minutes until cheese is bubbly.
5. **Serve:** Serve hot with a side of pasta.

Creamy Polenta with Mushrooms

Ingredients:

- 1 cup polenta
- 4 cups vegetable broth
- 1 cup heavy cream
- 1 tablespoon butter
- 2 cups mushrooms (sliced)
- 1/4 cup Parmesan cheese (grated)
- Salt and pepper to taste

Instructions:

1. **Cook Polenta:** Bring vegetable broth to a boil, then slowly whisk in polenta. Reduce heat and cook for 20-25 minutes, stirring often, until creamy.
2. **Sauté Mushrooms:** While the polenta cooks, sauté mushrooms in butter until golden and softened.
3. **Combine:** Stir heavy cream, Parmesan, and mushrooms into the polenta. Season with salt and pepper.
4. **Serve:** Serve the creamy polenta hot with extra Parmesan and fresh herbs.

Spaghetti and Meatballs

Ingredients:

- 1 lb spaghetti
- 1 lb ground beef
- 1/4 cup breadcrumbs
- 1/4 cup Parmesan cheese (grated)
- 1 egg
- 2 cloves garlic (minced)
- 1/2 cup parsley (chopped)
- 1 jar marinara sauce (about 24 oz)

- Salt and pepper to taste
- Olive oil for frying

Instructions:

1. **Make Meatballs:** In a bowl, combine ground beef, breadcrumbs, Parmesan, egg, garlic, parsley, salt, and pepper. Form into meatballs (about 1 inch in diameter).
2. **Cook Meatballs:** Heat olive oil in a skillet over medium heat. Brown meatballs in batches, cooking for 5-7 minutes, until browned on all sides.
3. **Simmer in Sauce:** Add marinara sauce to the skillet, reduce heat, and simmer for 15-20 minutes until meatballs are fully cooked.
4. **Cook Spaghetti:** While the meatballs cook, bring a large pot of salted water to a boil and cook the spaghetti according to package instructions.
5. **Serve:** Drain pasta and serve with meatballs and sauce on top. Garnish with additional Parmesan and parsley.

Risotto with Shrimp and Peas

Ingredients:

- 1 lb shrimp (peeled and deveined)
- 1 cup Arborio rice
- 4 cups chicken broth
- 1/2 cup white wine
- 1 small onion (chopped)
- 1 cup frozen peas
- 1/2 cup Parmesan cheese (grated)
- 2 tablespoons butter

- 2 tablespoons olive oil
- Salt and pepper to taste

Instructions:

1. **Cook Shrimp:** Heat olive oil in a large skillet over medium heat. Add shrimp and cook for 2-3 minutes per side until pink and cooked through. Remove and set aside.
2. **Cook Onions and Rice:** In the same skillet, add butter and sauté onion until softened. Stir in Arborio rice and cook for 1-2 minutes.
3. **Make Risotto:** Add white wine and stir until absorbed. Gradually add chicken broth, 1/2 cup at a time, stirring continuously until the liquid is absorbed before adding more. Continue until the rice is tender and creamy, about 20 minutes.
4. **Add Shrimp and Peas:** Stir in shrimp, peas, and Parmesan. Cook for 2-3 more minutes until heated through.
5. **Serve:** Season with salt and pepper to taste and serve immediately.

Roasted Chicken Thighs with Brussels Sprouts

Ingredients:

- 4 chicken thighs (bone-in, skin-on)
- 1 lb Brussels sprouts (trimmed and halved)
- 2 tablespoons olive oil
- 1 teaspoon garlic powder
- 1 teaspoon thyme
- Salt and pepper to taste
- 1 lemon (cut into wedges)

Instructions:

1. **Preheat Oven:** Preheat your oven to 400°F (200°C).
2. **Prepare Chicken and Brussels Sprouts:** Rub chicken thighs with 1 tablespoon olive oil, garlic powder, thyme, salt, and pepper. Toss Brussels sprouts with the remaining olive oil, salt, and pepper.
3. **Roast:** Arrange the chicken thighs on a baking sheet and surround them with Brussels sprouts. Roast for 35-40 minutes until the chicken is cooked through and the skin is crispy, and the Brussels sprouts are tender.
4. **Serve:** Squeeze lemon wedges over the chicken and Brussels sprouts before serving.

Vegetable Frittata

Ingredients:

- 6 eggs
- 1 cup milk
- 1 bell pepper (chopped)
- 1 small zucchini (sliced)
- 1/2 onion (chopped)
- 1 cup spinach (chopped)
- 1/2 cup shredded cheese (cheddar or mozzarella)
- 2 tablespoons olive oil

- Salt and pepper to taste

Instructions:

1. **Preheat Oven:** Preheat your oven to 375°F (190°C).
2. **Cook Vegetables:** In a skillet, heat olive oil over medium heat. Add bell pepper, zucchini, and onion, and cook until softened (about 5-7 minutes). Stir in spinach and cook until wilted.
3. **Prepare Egg Mixture:** In a bowl, whisk together eggs, milk, salt, and pepper.
4. **Combine:** Pour the egg mixture over the cooked vegetables in the skillet, and sprinkle with cheese.
5. **Bake:** Transfer the skillet to the oven and bake for 15-20 minutes, or until the eggs are set and the frittata is lightly golden.
6. **Serve:** Slice and serve warm.

Roast Beef with Yorkshire Pudding

Ingredients (Roast Beef):

- 3 lb beef roast (such as prime rib or top sirloin)
- 2 tablespoons olive oil
- 1 tablespoon rosemary (chopped)
- 1 tablespoon thyme (chopped)
- 4 cloves garlic (minced)
- Salt and pepper to taste

Ingredients (Yorkshire Pudding):

- 1 cup all-purpose flour
- 1 cup milk
- 4 large eggs
- 1/2 teaspoon salt
- 2 tablespoons vegetable oil

Instructions (Roast Beef):

1. **Preheat Oven:** Preheat your oven to 450°F (230°C).
2. **Season Beef:** Rub the beef roast with olive oil, rosemary, thyme, garlic, salt, and pepper.
3. **Roast Beef:** Place the roast on a rack in a roasting pan. Roast for 15 minutes, then reduce the temperature to 350°F (175°C). Continue roasting for 1-1.5 hours, or until the internal temperature reaches your desired doneness (130°F for medium-rare).
4. **Rest Beef:** Let the roast rest for 10-15 minutes before slicing.

Instructions (Yorkshire Pudding):

1. **Prepare Batter:** In a bowl, whisk together flour, milk, eggs, and salt until smooth.
2. **Preheat Pan:** Heat vegetable oil in a muffin tin or a large baking dish in the oven for about 10 minutes.
3. **Bake:** Pour the batter into the hot pan and bake for 20-25 minutes, or until golden and puffed.
4. **Serve:** Serve the roast beef with Yorkshire pudding and gravy.

Bacon-Wrapped Pork Tenderloin

Ingredients:

- 1 lb pork tenderloin
- 8 slices bacon
- 2 tablespoons olive oil
- 2 cloves garlic (minced)
- 1 tablespoon rosemary (chopped)
- Salt and pepper to taste

Instructions:

1. **Preheat Oven:** Preheat your oven to 375°F (190°C).
2. **Season Pork:** Rub the pork tenderloin with olive oil, garlic, rosemary, salt, and pepper.
3. **Wrap with Bacon:** Lay the bacon strips on a work surface and place the pork tenderloin in the center. Wrap the bacon around the pork, securing it with toothpicks if necessary.
4. **Roast Pork:** Place the bacon-wrapped pork in a roasting pan and bake for 25-30 minutes, or until the internal temperature reaches 145°F (63°C).
5. **Serve:** Let the pork rest for 5-10 minutes before slicing and serving.

Beef and Barley Soup

Ingredients:

- 1 lb beef stew meat (cut into cubes)
- 1 tablespoon olive oil
- 1 onion (chopped)
- 2 carrots (sliced)
- 2 celery stalks (chopped)
- 4 garlic cloves (minced)
- 1 cup barley
- 6 cups beef broth

- 1 bay leaf
- 1 teaspoon thyme
- Salt and pepper to taste

Instructions:

1. **Brown the Beef:** Heat olive oil in a large pot over medium heat. Add the beef stew meat and cook until browned on all sides. Remove and set aside.
2. **Sauté Vegetables:** In the same pot, add onion, carrots, celery, and garlic. Sauté for about 5 minutes until softened.
3. **Simmer Soup:** Add barley, beef broth, bay leaf, thyme, salt, and pepper to the pot. Bring to a boil, then reduce to a simmer.
4. **Cook the Soup:** Return the beef to the pot and simmer for 1-1.5 hours, until the beef is tender and the barley is cooked.
5. **Serve:** Remove the bay leaf, adjust seasoning if needed, and serve warm.

Pork and Apple Stew

Ingredients:

- 1 lb pork shoulder (cut into cubes)
- 2 tablespoons olive oil
- 1 onion (chopped)
- 2 apples (peeled and sliced)
- 2 carrots (sliced)
- 2 cloves garlic (minced)
- 4 cups chicken broth
- 1 teaspoon rosemary (chopped)

- 1 teaspoon thyme
- Salt and pepper to taste

Instructions:

1. **Brown the Pork:** Heat olive oil in a large pot over medium-high heat. Add pork cubes and brown on all sides. Remove and set aside.
2. **Sauté Vegetables:** In the same pot, sauté onion, carrots, and garlic until softened.
3. **Add Apples and Herbs:** Add apples, rosemary, thyme, salt, and pepper to the pot. Stir to combine.
4. **Simmer Stew:** Add chicken broth and pork back into the pot. Bring to a boil, then reduce to a simmer. Cover and cook for 1-1.5 hours until the pork is tender.
5. **Serve:** Taste and adjust seasoning if needed. Serve warm.

Braised Short Ribs

Ingredients:

- 4 beef short ribs
- 2 tablespoons olive oil
- 1 onion (chopped)
- 2 carrots (sliced)
- 2 celery stalks (chopped)
- 4 garlic cloves (minced)
- 1 cup red wine
- 3 cups beef broth

- 1 bay leaf
- 1 teaspoon thyme
- Salt and pepper to taste

Instructions:

1. **Brown the Ribs:** Heat olive oil in a large Dutch oven over medium-high heat. Season short ribs with salt and pepper, and brown on all sides. Remove and set aside.
2. **Sauté Vegetables:** In the same pot, sauté onion, carrots, celery, and garlic until softened.
3. **Deglaze:** Add red wine and cook for 3-4 minutes, scraping up any browned bits from the bottom of the pot.
4. **Braised Short Ribs:** Add beef broth, bay leaf, thyme, and short ribs back into the pot. Bring to a boil, then reduce to a simmer. Cover and braise in the oven at 350°F (175°C) for 2.5-3 hours, until the ribs are tender.
5. **Serve:** Remove the ribs and strain the sauce. Serve ribs with the sauce spooned over the top.

Chicken and Dumplings

Ingredients (for Soup):

- 1 lb chicken breasts (cooked and shredded)
- 1 onion (chopped)
- 2 carrots (diced)
- 2 celery stalks (diced)
- 4 cups chicken broth
- 1 teaspoon thyme
- 1 cup heavy cream
- Salt and pepper to taste

Ingredients (for Dumplings):

- 1 cup all-purpose flour
- 2 teaspoons baking powder
- 1/2 teaspoon salt
- 1/4 teaspoon pepper
- 1/4 cup butter (melted)
- 1/2 cup milk

Instructions:

1. **Make Soup:** In a large pot, sauté onion, carrots, and celery until softened. Add chicken broth, thyme, salt, and pepper. Bring to a boil and simmer for 10-15 minutes.
2. **Add Chicken and Cream:** Stir in shredded chicken and heavy cream. Adjust seasoning if needed.
3. **Make Dumplings:** In a bowl, combine flour, baking powder, salt, and pepper. Stir in melted butter and milk until just combined.
4. **Add Dumplings:** Drop spoonfuls of dumpling dough into the simmering soup. Cover the pot and simmer for 15-20 minutes, until the dumplings are cooked through.
5. **Serve:** Serve hot with extra seasoning if needed.

Sautéed Brussels Sprouts with Bacon

Ingredients:

- 1 lb Brussels sprouts (trimmed and halved)
- 4 slices bacon (chopped)
- 1 tablespoon olive oil
- 2 cloves garlic (minced)
- Salt and pepper to taste

Instructions:

1. **Cook Bacon:** In a large skillet, cook bacon over medium heat until crispy. Remove bacon and set aside, leaving bacon fat in the pan.
2. **Sauté Brussels Sprouts:** Add olive oil to the pan and heat over medium. Add Brussels sprouts and cook until golden brown and tender, about 8-10 minutes.
3. **Add Garlic and Bacon:** Add garlic and cook for another minute. Stir in cooked bacon, season with salt and pepper, and serve.

Pumpkin Risotto

Ingredients:

- 1 cup Arborio rice
- 1 small pumpkin (peeled, seeded, and cubed)
- 1/2 onion (chopped)
- 4 cups chicken or vegetable broth
- 1/2 cup white wine
- 1/2 cup Parmesan cheese (grated)
- 1 tablespoon butter
- 1 teaspoon sage (chopped)

- Salt and pepper to taste

Instructions:

1. **Cook Pumpkin:** In a saucepan, cook cubed pumpkin in a little water until tender, about 10 minutes. Puree until smooth.
2. **Sauté Onion and Rice:** In a large pan, sauté onion in butter until softened. Add Arborio rice and cook for 1-2 minutes.
3. **Make Risotto:** Add white wine and cook until absorbed. Gradually add broth, 1/2 cup at a time, stirring constantly until liquid is absorbed before adding more. Continue until rice is tender, about 20 minutes.
4. **Finish Risotto:** Stir in pureed pumpkin, Parmesan, sage, salt, and pepper. Cook for another 2-3 minutes.
5. **Serve:** Serve warm, garnished with additional Parmesan.

Tofu Stir-Fry with Rice

Ingredients:

- 1 block firm tofu (drained and cubed)
- 2 tablespoons soy sauce
- 1 tablespoon olive oil
- 1 bell pepper (sliced)
- 1 carrot (julienned)
- 1 zucchini (sliced)
- 2 cloves garlic (minced)

- 1 cup cooked rice
- 1 tablespoon sesame oil
- 1 tablespoon sesame seeds (optional)

Instructions:

1. **Prepare Tofu:** Press tofu to remove excess moisture, then cut into cubes.
2. **Sauté Tofu:** Heat olive oil in a skillet over medium heat. Add tofu cubes and cook until golden brown on all sides, about 8-10 minutes.
3. **Cook Vegetables:** In the same skillet, add bell pepper, carrot, zucchini, and garlic. Stir-fry for 5-7 minutes until vegetables are tender.
4. **Combine:** Add cooked rice and soy sauce, stir to combine. Cook for another 2-3 minutes.
5. **Finish and Serve:** Drizzle with sesame oil, sprinkle with sesame seeds, and serve warm.

www.ingramcontent.com/pod-product-compliance
Lightning Source LLC
LaVergne TN
LVHW081334060526
838201LV00055B/2641